T0146574

MY JOURNEY

BREAKING THE SILENCE FROM SHAME

IZORA D. SUMMERS

WestBow
PRESS®
A DIVISION OF THOMAS NELSON
& ZONDERVAN

Scripture taken from the New King James Version. Copyright © 1979, 1980, 1982 by Thomas Nelson, Inc. Used by permission. All rights reserved.

Scripture taken from the Holy Bible, NEW INTERNATIONAL VERSION®. Copyright © 1973, 1978, 1984 by Biblica, Inc. All rights reserved worldwide. Used by permission. NEW INTERNATIONAL VERSION® and NIV® are registered trademarks of Biblica, Inc. Use of either trademark for the offering of goods or services requires the prior written consent of Biblica US, Inc.

WestBow Press books may be ordered through booksellers or by contacting:

WestBow Press
A Division of Thomas Nelson & Zondervan
1663 Liberty Drive
Bloomington, IN 47403
www.westbowpress.com
1 (866) 928-1240

ISBN: 978-1-5127-4003-5 (sc)
ISBN: 978-1-5127-4002-8 (hc)
ISBN: 978-1-5127-4001-1 (e)

Library of Congress Control Number: 2016906804

Print information available on the last page.

WestBow Press rev. date: 05/12/2016

DEDICATION

To my son, Joshua. God does not make mistakes. When I brought you home, I thought I was saving you. Over the years, however, I learned that you saved me. You are a blessing. Always remember that you are a child of the Most High. You are destined for greatness.

Love, Mom

ACKNOWLEDGMENTS

Praise God, who is the beginning and the ending of everything that pertains to me. Thank you to the late Suffragan Bishop Cushinberry, who conducted a seminar on spiritual abuse at the Midwestern District Council of Christian Education. Mr. Adams, thank you for reminding me that this book is God's work. Sincere thanks to Dr. Stikes, who extends himself to counseling students and alumni at Missouri Baptist University. To my friends, blessings to you for your laughter, prayers, and listening ears. I am so grateful to God for my family, especially my mom, for saying, "Get that book finished!" You encouraged and supported me. Thank you for loving the woman I am becoming. Snow, I do not know where I would be in my process had it not been for the Lord using you. Thank you for not allowing me to stay silent by the shame.

FOREWORD

Have you ever wondered what happens to someone who is abused? What do people endure in their struggle to recover from shame? Wonder no more! *Breaking the Silence from Shame* is a must-read. Abuse has a horrific impact on its victims. Abuse causes a physical, visual, ritualistic, and spiritual affliction of destruction and shame. Izora provides an inside-out perspective that is a moving account that could only be done by someone who has been abused and knows the shame that could be so destructive that it never surfaces and heals. However, with God's grace and mercy, victims can survive and triumph. To God be the glory!

—Charles Scully Stikes, PhD

INTRODUCTION

When I kept silent my bones wasted away

through my groaning all day.

—Psalm 32:3

As I sat among the women and listened to their stories, I thought, *I'm in the wrong place.* In comparison to what these women had experienced, I had no right to be there. After all, I hadn't been sexually abused. Or had I? How in the world did I end up in a support group? All I had wanted was to be guided spiritually, not abused.

Their stories are tragic, yet not uncommon. The Rape, Abuse, and Incest National Network (RAINN) reported that one out of six women will experience some type of sexual abuse in her lifetime. How would a person know she has been abused? The American Heritage Dictionary, Second College Edition, defines the verb *abuse* as "to use wrongfully or improperly. To trick or to deceive. To hurt or injure by maltreatment. To assail with contemptuous, coarse or insulting words." Many women are not aware that a variety of sexual behaviors fall under the category of sexual abuse.

According to the workbook *Shelter from the Storm*, sexual abuse can be divided into several categories:

- Physical abuse: touching or fondling a child or adult without consent; excessive tickling; or physical restraint.
- Visual abuse: exposure to pornography without consent; forced manipulation or coercion to observe another masturbate; exposure of genitals to a nonconsenting child or adult.
- Verbal abuse: exposes a child or nonconsenting adult to sexual jokes, teasing, or graphic sexual descriptions; repeated remarks about a child's development; or refusing to allow a child privacy while dressing.

- Covert abuse: observing another person nude without their consent; or videotaping people having sex without their consent.

- Ritualistic sexual abuse: forcing a person to participate in religious activities that include sex; or forced sexual activity that involves chants or incantations.

Another type of abuse is spiritual abuse. In *The Subtle Power of Spiritual Abuse*, David Johnson and Jeff VanVonderen define spiritual abuse as the abusive treatment of a person who is in need of help, support, or greater spiritual empowerment, with the result of weakening, undermining, or decreasing that person's spiritual empowerment.

In the past, I had experienced some inappropriate behaviors: adolescent boys playing "catch a girl, get a girl," sexual comments made by a former supervisor, and being sexually propositioned by an adult cousin. But this situation seemed different. The only adjective I had to describe what had happened to me was *bizarre*. As I looked over the glossary on sexual abuse, I could not identify with it. I had welcomed Pastor Sale into my life, into my home. He had been my answer to some long-awaited prayers.

The way I reacted to what happened, I knew that I had never dealt with the ramifications of my cousin and former supervisor's actions toward me. Like many women, I just ignored it and went on about my business. Sexual assault is one of the most underreported crimes, with 68 percent still being left unreported (RAINN).

This book was born out of that pain and shame. It's not that my story is unusual. Unfortunately, thousands of stories just like mine exist; however, many are never told because of the shame.

Sharing my story is a part of my healing process. I pray that many other people will be free from the bondage of shame and guilt. My support group has helped me see that any time a person uses his authority to manipulate a situation, it's abuse. Whether it happens once or over a period of years, it's wrong.

Many times the victim will assume all the shame and guilt from the abuse, whereas the perpetrator goes on with his life. We internalize the ordeal and point the finger at ourselves as if we have done something wrong.

I'm glad that I have gotten past the torment of self-blame. You replay everything in your head thousands of times, wondering if you smiled too much, or maybe the clothes you had on that day were too revealing, or if only you'd not gone to his house.

The Bible reminds us that we have an enemy, the Devil, who prowls like a roaring lion looking for someone to devour (1 Peter 5:8). Sounds like a pedophile to me! I've had women ask me how I could allow such a thing to continue for so long. One woman suggested that the abuse was a result of past sin that I had committed. God said He is faithful and just and will forgive us our sins (1 John 1:9). What she didn't know was that I was no stranger to inappropriate touch. The enemy started to prey on me in my childhood.

A word to anyone reading this who may encounter someone who has been abused: focus on providing a listening ear. God will reveal in His time the *why* behind the *what*. Don't be like Job's friend Eliphaz and try to give a reason for the person's suffering.

According to RAINN, about one-third of child sexual abuse victims report experiencing repeated victimization, and sexual abuse victims have a two to three times greater risk of adult revictimization than women without a history of child sexual abuse. The Bible tells us that our struggle is not against flesh and blood, but against rulers, authority, the power of this dark world, and the spiritual forces of evil in the heavenly realms (Ephesians 6:12).

Familiar spirits and generational curses have been the subject of many books and sermons. Just as the color of people's eyes and skin and their hair texture can be passed down through generations, so can spirits. God let me know that the spirit of control was a familiar spirit. The Lord gave me an example of how familiar spirits operate, by having me to watch my dog. As I walked my dog, he would stop and sniff every four feet, with his tail wagging. He would lift up one of his short legs and mark his spot.

In showing me about familiar spirits, God led me to call a local veterinarian's office. According to the veterinarian, dogs have a keen sense that humans don't possess. The doctor said that dogs can't resist the urge to leave their mark. Their senses are so powerful that they can sense the sex of the other dog's urine. Many times they can tell how much time has passed since the previous dog was present. They can smell other types of urine, but they are interested only in their own species.

In the spiritual realm, a demonic spirit can tell what kind of spirit has been in operation. For example, if a spirit of control exists, there is potential for the spirit of dominance, possessiveness, and witchcraft to surface.

I write this book not to expose anyone, but rather to inform women and men of the abuse that occurs within our churches. I write in hopes that you will understand that the enemy wants to keep you silent. He wants to suffocate you with shame. He wants you to feel so worthless that you never go on to live a healthy, productive life. That's his job. He comes to steal, kill, and destroy. But Jesus came that you might have life, and have it more abundantly!

As a Christian and Licensed Professional Counselor, I write from multiple disciplines: spiritually, emotionally, and psychologically. I address the origins of shame, spiritual abuse, and traits of manipulation and trust between laymen and leadership. I use the word *him* as gender neutral when referring to the abuser.

Perhaps you have not admitted to being abused. A word of caution: if you decide to go through your journey toward healing, it will not be a pleasant process. I suggest prayer and asking God to lead you to people who can contain the various emotions that pour from your heart. At the end of this book, I have included references to additional resources, as well as questions to discuss among small groups.

As you read this book, know that you are not alone. God says He will never leave you or forsake you (Hebrews 13:5). He will be there as you work through your journey to breaking the silence from shame.

CHAPTER 1

A Seed Sown

Always seek out the seed of triumph in every adversity.

—Og Mandino

I asked Jesus into my life at the age of six. As a child, I heard many sermons about the imminent return of Jesus Christ and the rapture, and I did not want to be left behind. Perhaps my salvation at that time was more about fear than faith. Hebrews 10:3 says that faith comes by hearing the message, so what messages did I receive as a child in church? I admired my mother, who was an active member in the church, a Sunday school teacher, and an usher. I wanted to be like my mom.

I was raised Pentecostal, so I was taught that I would be saved when I received the baptism of the Holy Spirit. This confused me because I knew that I had asked Jesus into my heart and had been baptized in water. Nonetheless, according to the Pentecostal exegesis of Scripture, I was not saved. According to Romans 8:9 *(NKJV)*, "But you are not in the flesh but in the Spirit, if indeed the Spirit of God dwell in you. Now if anyone does not have the Spirit of Christ, he is not His." Speaking in tongues was considered to be evidence of the Holy Spirit, and I didn't speak in tongues. So I was not allowed to serve on auxiliaries in the church, although I was afforded the opportunity to participate in the Easter and Christmas programs.

For years I would "tarry" for the Holy Ghost, as did the early church on the day of Pentecost. There was no sound as a mighty rushing wind. I did however hear a woman shouting in my left ear, "Yeah, yeah, that's it. Keep going!" And another woman in my right ear, "Give it all to Him. Let it go!" Meanwhile, as instructed, I repeatedly said, "Hallelujah!" Many times I would leave the prayer room breathing heavily and wet from sweating. That experience led me to believe that I was doing something wrong—that somehow I was undeserving of God's Spirit inside of me. A seed was planted that would later grow into feelings of shame, which I will address in a later chapter. I know now that I was saved back then. I was His child. I was a part of the kingdom of God.

I am in no way discrediting the teachings that I received. People work with the knowledge they have. I respect and admire those women who labored with people to bring them closer to God. But I now believe that it was man's rule—not God's rule— that did not allow me to serve in the church. Jesus said, "Let the children alone, don't prevent them from coming to me. God's kingdom is made up of people like these" (Matthew 19:14 *MSG*).

I wasn't asking to be a leader or to preach; I just wanted to be an usher like my mom. I sat and watched my friends serve on the junior usher board, and I wanted to do the same. Every so often I heard about a church friend who received the Holy Spirit, and I fumed with jealousy and resentment. But as I got older, my preoccupation with serving on the usher board diminished. I started to see troubling things—those same girls who had been *saved* were also dancing, cursing, and having sex, according to conversations we would have in the women's restroom. But the Devil had already made his deposit in me: insecurity.

CHAPTER 2

My Shame

Shame is a soul-eating emotion.

—C. G. Jung

Sexual improprieties go back to biblical times. One familiar story is that of Tamar and Amnon in the third chapter of 2 Samuel. Tamar, then fifteen, was raped by her half-brother Amnon, who was thirty-two. The Bible says that Amnon was so distracted over his sister that he became sick. He had a friend named Jonadab, who was a very crafty man. This Jonadab could be a type of Satan—a crafty and cunning man who told Amnon what to do and how to do it.

Tamar, like many victims of child molestation, was being submissive to her father, King David. He told her to go and prepare a meal for her brother. Amnon ordered everyone out of the room except Tamar and asked her to lie with him. She asked that he not do such a disgraceful thing. According to the National Child Traumatic Stress Network, more than half of children who are sexually abused are victims of a parent or relative. Perhaps you have experienced feelings of degradation. Tamar asked, "Where can I take my shame?" Like many people who accept shame, she felt as though something was wrong with her.

During biblical times, being with a man other than your husband was considered immoral, and women who were forced to do so were shunned for their behavior. In Ronald Potter-Efron and Patricia Potter-Efron's book *Letting Go of Shame*, the authors explain that shame can be culturally driven. The culture of the Jewish people was based on virtue.

Unfortunately Tamar didn't have a Bible, so she couldn't find comfort in verses such as these:

> Cast all your anxiety on Him because He cares for
> you. (1 Peter 5:7)

Do not be afraid; you will not suffer shame. Do
not fear disgrace; you will not be humiliated. You
will forget the shame of your youth. (Isaiah 54:4)

That is why I am suffering as I am. Yet this is no
cause for shame, because I know whom I have
believed, and am convinced that he is able to
guard what I have entrusted to him for that day.
(2 Timothy 1:12)

Come to me, all you who are weary and burdened,
and I will give you rest. (Matthew 11:28)

I often tell people that the long-term effect of what happened
to me was more atrocious than the actual act. It robbed me of my
joy, peace, and communion with God. When Amnon told Tamar
to get out, sending her away was more damaging in the long term
than the rape itself.

Not only did Tamar have to deal with the shame, but she was
also silenced. Her brother Absalom asked her if Amnon had been
with her. Then he said to her, "But now hold your peace, my sister.
He is your brother; do not take this thing to heart" (2 Samuel 13:20
NKJV). The Bible does not speak of Tamar after that, but verse 23

says that it was a full two years before her brother Absalom took action.

Thankfully, God would not allow me to keep silent. It was imperative that I begin the healing process immediately. Why? you may wonder. Because I had to be in sync with God's timing. A season was coming when people like you would need to hear my story, so that they could understand His grace toward me. My prayer for you is that you do not wait. Whether it happened fifteen years ago or last night, don't carry the burden alone—give it to Jesus. God will direct you.

God put someone in my life years ago whom I felt I could confide about personal matters. That person gave me twenty-four hours to make a decision. Either I would go to the senior pastor, she would go with me to the senior pastor, or she would go alone to the senior pastor. How would I explain to the pastor what had happened? I worried. Several scenarios played out in my mind like a movie, but all of them made me feel inadequate. I should have known better, I kept thinking.

Most people occasionally experience shame. Shame is a part of life, and moderate shame can help you develop as a person. But there are important differences between shame and guilt. Shame points the finger at your being, and guilt focuses more on your actions. Shamed people think that something is wrong with them. In contrast, guilty people believe that they only need to correct their wrong actions.

A shamed person fears abandonment; a guilty person fears punishment. Shamed people do not like or respect themselves, and they believe that others see them as they see themselves—as imperfect people. A shamed person sabotages relationships by anticipating that other people will leave as soon as they realize that the shamed person is flawed.

Healing from guilt is easier than healing from shame, because shame is about the person rather than about that person's actions. A shamed person heals by learning to view himself or herself as a person of worth and value.

How do people know they are experiencing feelings of shame? I can recall two times in my life when I had this indefinable feeling. How do I now know that I was experiencing shame? According to Potter-Efron, shame has specific characteristics: a strong physical response, uncomfortable thoughts, troublesome behavior, and spiritual agony.

Shame is also very much a mental process. Sometimes we cannot stop thinking about our embarrassments, defeats, and humiliations. Those moments seem like they go on forever, and we end up calling ourselves terrible names such as *stupid, dummy,* or *idiot.*

Shame involves a failure of the total being. People who are ashamed believe that they should not exist. It's not that they have done anything wrong—again, that would be guilt, not shame. Shamed people believe that *they are* what is wrong—that *they are* shame. Shamed people often experience a spiritual crisis, perhaps thinking that even God has forsaken them. They may feel unworthy of love, according to the Potter-Efrons.

When we lose our connections with our higher power, we become isolated from all external sources of comfort. We can feel a tremendous loneliness at the center of our being. A feeling of emptiness is accompanied by feelings of worthlessness. The shamed woman often feels hollowed out. Her identity has been compromised. Like foundation conceals a person's flaws, the abused woman smiles to cover her shame and hide her emptiness.

Shame has five possible sources or origins: the biological shame, shame and the family of origin, current shaming relationships, societal pressures that activate shame, and shaming adults.

A young girl raised among family members who have constantly criticized her may feel that she is not good enough or pretty enough. If they are concerned about their image and what the neighbors think, family members will learn to keep up the facade or else face punishment. Children who grow up in this environment usually grow up to be shaming adults who feel worthless.

Institutions such as workplaces, churches, and schools bear some responsibility for providing the kind of structure that ensures dignity, but they can also contribute to a person's shame. Instead of providing strong goals and appropriate boundaries, sometimes they are organized in a way that shrinks individuals. Then the resulting shame brings depth to spiritual despair, according to Ronald and Patricia Potter-Efron.

As mentioned in the previous chapter, I grew up in a traditional Pentecostal church. Showing bare arms and legs, going to movies, listening to secular music, and wearing makeup were not acceptable for saints. The origin of my shame was a spiritual identity crisis. I didn't know who I was in Christ. Sometimes when people outside my denomination asked if I was saved, I did not know how to answer the question, and I stumbled over my words.

While in high school, I was a member of a gospel choir that sang at various churches. At one singing engagement, as I recall, the Spirit of God was strong and choir members were screaming and shouting and running around. I left the pulpit, found an empty room, and fell to my knees, asking God to fill me with His Spirit. I cried and asked, "God, what is wrong with me? Why don't I feel what they are feeling? Why can't I jump and shout?" I knew that many choir members were from other denominations that didn't teach about the infilling of the Holy Spirit, and yet those choir members felt His presence. I was confused and unsure of my spirituality.

At that time, members of Pentecostal churches were known as the *sanctified* or *holy rollers*. First Thessalonians says that we should be sanctified, which means to be set apart, and the Bible encourages us to be holy (Hebrews 12:14). When someone started to jump or shout, non-Pentecostals would say, "She caught the Holy Ghost." It's true that the Spirit of God can certainly make people jump and run around, but so can being at a rhythm and blues concert! More than that, the Spirit of God is about power— power to love, deliver, heal, and forgive.

Mrs. Carter, eighty years old, tells about when she felt shamed in the church as a young woman. According to Mrs. Carter, the teaching at her church was to date someone of the same faith. Mrs. Carter was saved, but she fell in love with a man who was not attending church at the time. She recalls that she married this man without counsel from her pastor. Mrs. Carter says that after she got married, she was "sat down" from singing in the choir and was not allowed to serve the church in any capacity, all because she had married someone who was not saved. Mrs. Carter sat for three years, and the new pastor told her that it was time for her to get up and serve God.

When asked about feelings of shame, Mrs. Carter says that she did not question the pastor's decision to sit her down, because she knew what the church taught. But she continued to attend church because she had a desire to get closer to God. She said that her church friends included her in social outings, but on Sunday mornings when the choir sang, she felt left out and lonely.

Mrs. Carter says she desired her husband to attend church. However, she saw men come to church and get saved only so that they could marry the women of the church, and many of those relationships did not last. Mrs. Carter says that her decision to marry someone outside of church is a choice with which she has had to live. But God has been merciful to her, and she has been married to the same man for fifty-five years. Perhaps if the church had shown love to Mrs. Carter and her husband, he would have come to Christ and she would not have felt so lonely. Mrs. Carter says that one of her missions is to encourage people who feel like they are not a part of the church, to let them know that they have value in the kingdom of God.

Shame breeds secrecy. Shame is a painful emotion caused by a strong sense of guilt, embarrassment, unworthiness, and disgrace. As born-again Christians, we are alerted by the Holy Spirit, through our conscience, when we sin. The problem is that many times the victim can't tell the difference between shame and actual sin. We feel shame because we assume responsibility for our perpetrator's actions.

I felt very responsible for the removal of Pastor Sale. I kept silent and listened while people expressed their disapproval of his termination. Of course, they knew only that he had broken the rule about not going to a woman's house alone.

I would sit in church and feel as if I had a scarlet letter printed on my chest. The other associate pastors knew what happened, and I felt as though they were trying to keep their distance from me. Had I not said anything, the church would still have one of its pastors.

A month after his dismissal, I felt in my spirit the Lord leading me to share with the prayer team I'd served on what happened to me. There were too many unanswered questions among them. I didn't want them to have any ill feelings toward the Board of Directors for the decision they made.

Many of the people on the team looked up to this man. Like me, they admired him and desired to be used of God as the Lord used him. Although I was nervous, God gave me peace that it was the right thing to do. He promised that by exposing myself and telling the truth, I would not be subjecting myself to open shame. He would be in the midst of the situation.

When I shared my story with the team, I shook. I didn't look up. I didn't want people seeing my eyes, a common physical trait of shame. Afterward, some people thanked me for coming forth. Others said they felt free, and some cried. They knew that if not for the grace of God, they too could have been one of his victims. After the meeting the senior pastor and his wife talked with those who wanted to continue to discuss what had happened. The pastor said to me that God had something special in store for me. Although I appreciated those words, I wasn't too convinced.

Several weeks later, I received the following letter from Stacey, one of the ministers who attended the meeting:

> Thank you for having the courage to come forward and share what happened to you. Often people talk about "carrying our cross" and sharing in the suffering of Jesus. Many times we think of it only in terms of sharing the Gospel with others, having to endure verbal attacks on our faith,

or risk people rejecting us because of what we believe. But you exemplified what it means to be a Christian.

You carried a heavy burden on your heart and almost walked away from the church and the prayer team, but instead you told someone else what happened, and it helped the Body of Christ. You could have stopped there, but you went further and admitted to the prayer team that you were the person that it happened to. You stepped forward, not knowing if anyone would understand, but you did it for yourself and to help others so there would be no questions. That is bearing your cross. You risked everything to share the truth. Not to destroy, but to build up.

Know that because of your honesty and transparency before God that you not only blessed our church, but you will be able to set free many others who are bound by secrets that are too heavy for them to bear alone.

Although the letter was very encouraging, I already had filtered out any positive feedback and was focused on my own negative thoughts about myself instead. I felt exposed and ashamed. Only twelve people had attended the meeting, but those twelve had friends whom they would tell, and so forth. By the end of the week, the entire congregation would know that I was the reason for Pastor Sale's dismissal. This was part of my distorted thinking process. In counseling we call this *forecasting.* I had shared with the team, and now I was predicting an outcome.

I continued to work in the ministry, facilitating support groups, teaching classes, and praying for people at the altar. Each time I walked into the sanctuary, the whispering demons told me that people were thinking, *How could she have been so stupid?* This wasn't hard to believe, since I said it to myself a thousand times a day. Again, I was engaged in distorted thinking, assuming that I could read people's minds.

For my healing from shame to take place, I had to acknowledge those distorted thoughts. I had to practice self-talk, saying realistic or positive statements to myself. I had to be mindful of the negative thoughts that I allowed myself to think. When I started to think that I wasn't qualified to pray for people, I would have to bring that thought into captivity with the Word of God. "Those He predestined, he also called; he justified. He also glorified" (Romans 8:30). Before the foundation of the world, God had already qualified me to be where I was, doing what He called me to do. I had to stop those nagging, negative thoughts and replace them with something positive.

One technique I used to help improve my self-esteem was to look into a mirror and say aloud what I saw reflecting back at me. I would focus on my positive attributes instead of those things I wanted to change. I also surrounded myself with people who affirmed my self-worth in Christ. My liberation from shame came in knowing that God has a place for me in the kingdom of God, and that the same power that raised Jesus from the dead resides inside of me. Jesus gave me just what I needed when I needed it. He knew of my dependency on those in spiritual authority, and yet the Creator of the Universe still loved me.

Let's place the blame where it belongs: on the Devil. Don't hold on to the shame. Jesus loves you, and He has already set you free from the law of sin and death. God is waiting to take your shame and guilt. He is close to the downtrodden. You are not alone. You have value. Healing from shame takes time and patience. An open wound doesn't heal overnight, no matter how much medication you apply to the area. As a matter of fact, applying too much may have an adverse effect. So it is with shame. Shame heals slowly. You must become fully aware of your shame, notice your indicators of shame, and investigate the source.

CHAPTER 3

Spiritual Abuse

The greater the power, the more dangerous the abuse.

—Edmund Burke

This is perhaps the most difficult chapter of all to write. This abuse, unlike my previous experiences, left me for dead spiritually.

For years I have kept a personal journal. Based on what I wrote at the time, it's obvious that I thought Pastor Sale was an answer to prayer. "April 04. I thank You for not forgetting about me. I thank You because You have heard my prayer. Pastor Sale said that he is to pour more into my life. God, thank You for surrounding me with anointed people."

I was at a place in my walk with God where I needed to know my purpose and destiny. Within a twelve-month period, I had become an adopted parent, bought a house, lost a job, and been given a medical diagnosis. I came to my new church wanting and needing a spiritual parent, ready to walk in the call that was on my life. I needed guidance. I needed to learn how to submit to authority and leadership because I was someone who tended to speak my mind. I lacked respect for two professions that serve and protect, police and pastors.

There were many associate pastors at the church, along with the senior pastor. This particular associate pastor seemed to take an interest in my spiritual well-being, and I was in awe of how God moved in his life. When he prayed for people, he wasn't loud, and people would shake as though they had been hit by a bolt of lightning. Sometimes he would just walk past people and they would fall back.

In Christendom, this is what is called being *slain in the spirit.* I wanted to learn all that I could under his leadership. I was honored that God would place an anointed person in my life.

Growing up, I had a very wise pastor. It was not until he passed that I began my quest for purpose. The pastor after him did his best. He told me that God had a plan for my life, but he never gave me any details or hints about what that plan might be.

By this time I had received the infilling of the Holy Spirit and worked on several auxiliaries in the church, but I felt that there was something more that I was to do. I read books on spiritual gifts, deliverance, and recognizing the voice of God. A friend teased me, asking, "How many books on the same topic do you need?" I knew that I was *spiritually pregnant* with purpose and whatever it was would not give me rest. A woman carrying a baby feels the baby moving and kicking, often causing her some discomfort as the baby stretches and presses against her organs.

I frequently dreamed about being pregnant. In one dream that I remember vividly, my stomach looked like I was about five months pregnant. I felt a dark presence in front of me. I knew that it was a man, and his hands were gripping my stomach, squeezing my stomach to the point of agony. I woke up to that pain. Now I realize that the dream was spiritual, because I have never been pregnant with a child. The enemy was trying to abort my purpose, which was in my spirit. This purpose that I was carrying was bigger than me. It was stretching me, cultivating the fruit of the Spirit: love, joy, peace, patience, kindness, goodness, faithfulness, gentleness, and self-control.

Here's my journal entry from May 04: "God is so faithful. He does not forget our prayers. Pastor Sale said that the Lord has told him to under shepherd me and that he was going to pour into my life. I told him that I wanted him to help me to cultivate any gifts that are lying dormant."

Things started off wonderfully. It was the best of times and the worst of times, because I was still unemployed and a parent. My crisis stirred up a desire to seek God, so I was at church most of the time. When I wasn't there, Pastor Sale called to check on me. When I was having a bad day unbeknownst to him, he would call and tell me that the Lord had him up praying for me. I was just so grateful to God.

During this time, I was experiencing some pain in my arms and legs. I'd been to the doctor and had some blood work done. The test results showed that my body was producing small levels of antinuclear antibodies that indicated lupus, an autoimmune disease. At that time, the doctor wasn't concerned; he explained the disease and several studies that had been done on lupus. He said that perhaps I was one of those people who produced small levels, but he could not promise that I would not get sick.

I made the mistake of going online and looking up everything I could about lupus. I learned that lupus could cause anything from a mild attack on the joints to death. So instead of focusing on my mild symptoms, I began to experience anxiety about possibly getting seriously ill—which kept me up at night.

I cried out to God like never before. I now know that stress from the possibility of getting sick exacerbated my symptoms. I prayed and believed that God could totally heal me, but the pain in my arms and legs was excruciating. So when the pastor told me that God wanted to give him the gift of healing, I was all ears.

The abuse was subtle. Pastor Sale would come over to talk to me and help with small jobs around my house. The church rule was that men were not to visit women's homes alone. I knew this, but I assumed that the church staff was aware of our meetings. When I mentioned this to Pastor Sale, he said that he wasn't concerned about me causing any problems for him, and so our visits continued. On one visit, he asked for a hug, to make sure that I was okay spiritually. I stepped into his stretched-out arms and he hugged me tightly, not saying a word. What was he sensing? He later told me that he had sensed the pain in my body.

Over the next several weeks, he and I had many discussions on spiritual matters. Again, I felt privileged to be graced with the presence of this anointed man of God. I was starting to look to him as the kind of spiritual father I had always wanted. My parents were involved in my life, but I was seeking assurance that

I had a place in the kingdom of God. This pastor told me just what I wanted to hear, that God wanted to use me in a great way.

Later he said that the Lord told him to anoint me. In biblical times, when a person was anointed with oil, it was usually to set them apart for a particular assignment from God. Moses anointed Aaron and his sons to be priests, and Samuel anointed Saul to be king. Pastor Sale said that my anointing was to protect me and to prepare me for ministry.

The day that he was to pray for me, he came over to my house with a special blend of oils. He told me to change into something that I wouldn't mind getting stained. He looked around the house and said that we should go down into the basement, because if someone saw him, he or she would not understand. In the basement, he told me to lie on the floor. Dressed in my sports bra and biking shorts, my body lay on the cold concrete floor. On his knees, he positioned himself between my legs and rubbed oil all over my body. I closed my eyes and focused on being healed. Periodically I would open my eyes just to see what he was doing. His eyes were closed and there was sweat rolling down his face. He didn't say a word as he continued to rub. I jumped up when I felt oil trickle down my pelvis, and wrapped my hand around his wrist to stop him. He said that he saw in the Spirit that I was having some female problems. He also told me that the enemy was trying to kill me, but not to worry because he wasn't going to let anything happen to me.

We had three anointing sessions over the course of two months. Pastor Sale told me that the Lord instructed him to rub oil on me, but I began to wonder. After all, according to my latest blood work, my lupus was in remission, and I was healed.

He told me that he saw something going on with my feet. For that session, we did not go to the basement; instead, he had me lie on the floor of my eight-by-five bathroom. My head was pressed against the tub and my legs extended out the door. The pastor once again positioned himself between my legs and rubbed oil all over my body—legs, thighs, arms, stomach, and chest.

Deciphering the truth was hard because I had other people telling me they saw pain in certain parts of my body. When I started my journey toward healing, I learned that one thing that makes deception so effective is that it usually contains some element of truth. Our job is to figure out which part is true, but even then we must go to the Word of God to find answers and begin to pray.

Prophecy is defined as speaking forth or foretelling the will and counsel of God. God can give personal prophecies today, just as He did in biblical times. In 2 Samuel 12:13, for example, Nathan prophesy to David. And in Acts 11:28, Agabus predicts that a severe famine will spread over the entire Roman world.

In Isaiah 38, King Hezekiah was deathly ill. The prophet Isaiah went to the king and told him that the Lord said to get his house in order, because he was going to die. Now, I'm sure the king Hezekiah respected the prophet; however, the Bible says that Hezekiah turned his face toward the wall and prayed.

This *wall* can symbolize our secret place. Jesus said in Matthew 6:6, "When we pray to go into our room and shut the door and pray to the Father who is in the secret place and the Father, who is in the secret place will reward you openly." In his prayer, Hezekiah reminded God how he walked in truth and with a loyal heart. Then the prophet Isaiah came back and told Hezekiah that the Lord had heard him and was adding fifteen years to his life.

There are many operations to a gift: symbols, gestures, or words. God may use a person through art, dance, music or words. God is not limited to one way of getting His message to people. Many times the Lord has already been dealing with the person about the situation. The prophecy should not try to control a person, rob him or her of free will, or cause confusion or anxiety.

Prophecy is like a two-sided coin. First Corinthians 13:9 tells us, "We prophecy in part." We don't have the whole picture, so every believer has a responsibility to petition God about both sides of the coin. We are to ask for wisdom and clarity, beyond the prophecy itself. Finally, when you get a prophecy from someone, do as Mary, the mother of Jesus, did. She pondered the message that was given to her and kept it in her heart. Write down the word given, date it, and pray over it. I encourage you to keep a prayer journal. It's good to be able to read back and reflect, and it also helps to build your faith.

I didn't realize it then, but my spirit was alarming me about the actions of Pastor Sale. Any time you don't have true peace about a situation, it's probably the Lord trying to warn you. I've been in church all of my life, but I had never seen or heard of any pastor anointing people in this manner. I rationalized that Jesus had used unconventional ways to heal people. For example, Elijah lay on a boy three times (I Kings 18:21), Elisha sent a word for Naaman to wash in the Jordan River seven times (2 Kings 5:10), and Jesus put spit on a blind man's eyes (Mark 8:23). Who was I to question the ways of God?

Also during this time, Pastor Sale told me to change my diet and not eat certain foods. He asked me how much I loved God.

Then he told me to consecrate myself, and said that no one was to pray for me except a select few people, including him. He also told me that if I needed a massage, I was not to go to a spa—he would do it for me.

Several months went by, and my spirit was restless. I questioned the pastor's motives for being so kind to me. Why was I being given so much attention? There was a knot in my stomach because I sensed that this pastor would eventually want me to do something for him. What that would be, I wasn't certain. But what had originally seemed to be a blessing from God had now turned into a nightmare.

The last time Pastor Sale came to my house, he said that the Lord wanted him to pray for me. He asked me to take off as many of my clothes as possible. For the first time, I told him that I didn't feel like removing my clothes. We talked about something else for a while. Then suddenly he said that he had come to my house to transfer the power to me, and that what I did afterward was up to me. Immediately I heard in my spirit the word *manipulation*.

I had heard of manipulation, but it was not a word that I would use in my everyday vernacular to describe someone's actions. According to "Inside the Manipulator's Mind," a seminar conducted by Alan Godwin, manipulators are deficient in the *vitamins* that help them to be reasonable people, such as empathy, humility, awareness, responsibility, and reliability. Someone who practices manipulative techniques keeps up the drama and is good at masking his or her public and personal life. Manipulators will push your buttons to get a reaction out of you, only to use it against you. As was true in my case, manipulators also will use emotional blackmail. That's when someone punishes you for not doing what he or she wants you to do. That person knows how much you value the relationship, and he or she uses that against you. Manipulators change only because of some external situation, not because they recognize their own need to change.

When dealing with a manipulator, you may experience times when you feel crazy or question your own character. This is a trick of the manipulator, to turn the situation around to make you feel as though you have done something wrong. Manipulators know how to make you feel both good and bad, all at the same time.

People who find themselves falling prey to manipulators usually are vulnerable. They have naive expectations and want to think the best of all people. They try to reason with the unreasonable. The manipulator believes that his perception of things is reality, so he is unlikely to accept responsibility for any actions that would bring his character into question. The victim experiences confusion, because the manipulator is crafty. As long as you stay in your role, everything is okay. But as soon as you begin to question him or step out of the roles that he has established, that creates a problem.

After the pastor's last visit to my house, I was devastated. The eyes of my understanding had been opened. Just to go along with him, I told him that he could come back the next week. But when he left my house, I lay on the floor and curled up in a fetal position. A moan echoed from the deepest part of my being. Because I had refused to take my clothes off, he would not pray for me.

In my research on anointing and healings, I found a book on spiritual rituals. The words leaped out at me. The author of this book wrote of her experiences with the occult, and told about a healing ritual they had done. These meetings were usually held in remote areas. The high-ranking leader told the person in need of healing to relax, and the person and the leader would go to a tent to be alone. The leader would then *transmit* energy by laying her index finger on the person needing healing. Afterward, she would tell the person to lie down for a few hours for the process to begin.

Was I dreaming? What I was reading sounded all too familiar. But how could this be? Perhaps it was just a coincidence? Although

I am not suggesting that Pastor Sale was practicing witchcraft, I want to point out how we can take something sacred and defile it.

If we don't allow God to completely empty us, we can be left with residual aspects of our old lifestyle—gossiping, stealing, conning, or control. Spiritual abuse occurs to people of every race, economic class, and marital status. You've heard of its presence in various cults, but it is also occurring in many of our mainstream churches. And it often occurs in subtle ways. For me, there was no rape kit or forensic interviewing after what happened to me. The only evidence was the hole in my soul and the stain on my couch from the oil that was poured on me.

My journey to healing began the first time I heard the term *spiritual abuse*. To help me understand the dynamics of abuse in the church, I read *The Subtle Power of Spiritual Abuse*, by David Johnson and Jeff VanVonderen. Spiritual abuse occurs when someone is treated in a way that damages them spiritually. As defined in *The Subtle Power of Spiritual Abuse*, it is the maltreatment of a person who is in need of help, support, or greater spiritual empowerment, with the result of weakening, undermining, or decreasing that person's spiritual empowerment.

Spiritual abuse inflicted by a leader often exhibits classic characteristics. Sometimes a leader uses his position to control or dominate another person. For example, he might say, "Don't question me. I'm the pastor." Sometimes spirituality is used to force people to live up to certain standards of diet, clothing, and so on. Real needs are often neglected in favor of the needs of authority, and spirituality becomes more legalistic and less about resting in God. I remember feeling anxious about the diet that the pastor suggested. I was worried about failing before I even started the diet plan.

Victims of spiritual abuse usually struggle in the following areas. I was able to identify with several of these:

- Victims have a distorted image of God. For a while, I was very angry with God. How could He have allowed this to happen? And why was He still using this man in ministry? I was estranged from God. I didn't—couldn't—communicate with Him.

- Victims have a distorted self-identity as Christians. I didn't know who I was in Christ before the abuse, and after the abuse, I was confused about what I thought God was calling me to do.

- Victims have a hard time with God's grace. I knew the Word of God said that He would forgive, but I wasn't feeling God's grace or mercy. I believed that I had brought this on myself. Shame had overshadowed grace for me.

- Victims have difficulty with personal responsibility. They sometimes give up, or they put in just enough effort to get by. I was guilty of this. If a preacher or minister was around, I wanted to let them do the praying, visit the sick, and witness to the lost. I just wanted to attend church, pay my tithes, and then go home and mind my own business.

- Victims suffer from a lack of living skills. Although I couldn't readily relate to this area, I've witnessed people who could not function outside the structure of the church. While living on church grounds, they can live victorious lives. They are told when to pray, when to study, what to eat, and what to watch on television. Church programs need structure and order, but they should include life skills and emphasize self-discipline and integrity. Similarly, people released from prison sometimes have a difficult time reentering society, because they no longer have guards watching over them, telling them what to do and when to do it. With freedom comes much responsibility.

- Victims have a hard time admitting the abuse. They feel like they are the problem, as if they have been disloyal to the church, their families, or God. They lose track of what is normal. To call what has happened to them *spiritual abuse* seems crazy or exaggerated. This was me. I could not describe what happened to me. I was able to talk about the details, but I could not package it and put a label on it.

- Victims have a hard time trusting others. Those of us who have been abused spiritually have a hard time trusting the spiritual system. We know that it's vital to our Christian walk to be linked to a healthy, functioning church, but that takes time—and I'm still learning. However, God will provide a genuine man or woman of God whom you will be able to trust again.

Perhaps you're reading this and having a hard time with the term *spiritual abuse,* but the Bible speaks very clearly and concisely about leaders who mistreat God's sheep. In Jeremiah 5:26–29 (MSG) we read the following:

> My people are infiltrated by wicked man, unscrupulous men on the hunt. They set traps for the unsuspecting. Their victims are innocent men and women. Their houses are stuffed with ill-gotten gain, like hunter's bag full of birds.

Pretentious, powerful and rich, hugely obese, oily with rolls of fat. Worse, they have no conscience. Right and wrong means nothing to them. They stand up for no one, throw orphans to the wolves, and exploit the poor. Do you think I'll stand by and do nothing about this? Do you think I'll take serious measures against a people like this?

In Ezekiel 34:2-9 (MSG), the Lord told the prophet Ezekiel to warn the shepherds of Israel: "Doom to you shepherds of Israel, feeding your own mouths! Aren't shepherds supposed to feed sheep? You don't build up the weak ones, don't heal the sick, don't doctor the injured, don't go after the strays, don't look for the lost. You bully and badger them. And now they're scattered every which way because there is no shepherd-scattered and easy pickings for wolves and coyotes. Scattered-*my sheep*!-exposed and vulnerable across mountains and hills. My sheep scattered all over the world, and no one out looking for them."

If you have been spiritually abused, God has a promise just for you. He said that He is your shepherd, and He's coming to look for you. You may feel ashamed, guilty, and lost, but He's going to bring you back from the foreign people, your abusers. He said He will feed you on the mountains. He will take you out of the valley and set you up on high. You're going to eat in the rich pastures, because God's going to give you the nourishment that you need, and plenty of rest. He will come in and set things right.

For healing to take place from any abuse, you must first acknowledge that something has happened. Once you have done this, you can begin to work the process, which I will discuss in the upcoming chapters.

CHAPTER 4

Denial

The conflict between the will to deny horrible

events and the will to proclaim them aloud is the

central dialectic of psychological trauma.

—Judith L. Herman, *Trauma and Recovery*

Denial is a refusal to grant the truth of the statement of allegation. I sat in a room with women who had been molested by their fathers, their husbands, or strangers. Why was I there? At the age of fourteen, an adult cousin told me what boys would do to me as he pinned me up against the door with his body. At the age of twenty-one, I experienced sexual harassment on my job; I received unwanted hugs daily, and my paycheck was presented before me on my supervisor's desk, along with a condom. Both incidents I put out of my mind. Doesn't the Bible say to forget those things that are in the past?

I sat in that room with a heavy heart, trying to figure it all out. I usually don't talk much in front of strangers, but I found myself telling my story. I guess I hoped that the faster I talked, the sooner I'd be over it. As mentioned in previous chapters, however, it takes time to heal from shame, and patience must be exercised.

Gasps and looks of compassion were sent my way when I finished. A hush was in the air, and then I heard, "You were abused, and he used something as sacred as prayer to do it." I thought, *Abuse? I didn't say that!* It couldn't have been abused, because he had confessed to the Board of Directors and said that he just wanted me to be well and to operate in ministry. It's not as though I was a child being forced or coerced. I was an adult who willingly opened the door. The Lord let me know that in many regards, I was like a child. I looked to this man for my identity. I didn't know who I was in Christ.

I hadn't discovered the precious treasures that God had placed inside of me. I had searched for God, became impatient, and then turned to man. I couldn't understand why these women, whom I didn't know, were so angry. Was it because of the issues that they were facing? After all, it wasn't as if I had been raped. Or had I? I had been spiritually raped. What was taken from me wasn't physical, but it was spiritual. It left me feeling hollow inside, as though something had been methodically carved out of me.

To accept that something had happened to me, I had to face reality. As long as I stayed in denial, I didn't have to deal with myself or my emotions. To accept the truth meant that I would feel those strong emotions. Elisabeth Kubler-Ross is known for coining five stages of grief: denial, bargaining, anger, depression, and acceptance. These stages create a framework for understanding grief. There is no set order for grieving, and some people don't go through each step. I mention grief because when you have been abused, you experience a sense of loss.

According to *Shelter from the Storm*, sexual abuse does not have to be physical. Sexual abuse often begins with noncontact that invades a person emotionally, mentally, and spiritually. I trusted and admired Pastor Sale. I believed that he saw me like a daughter whom he was trying to help. I was in denial for about a month. As I attended group meetings to work through *Shelter from the Storm*, I discovered that what happened actually had a great effect on me.

My symptoms were similar to those of a person who had been physically raped. I felt empty, and I cried a lot and experienced anxiety attacks. I felt shame, guilt, fear, and anger. However, what concerned me the most was that I was withdrawing spiritually. I continued to go to church, but my soul wasn't there. I was born and raised in church, so I knew how to act. I went through all the formalities—lifting my hands and shouting, "Amen"—but I was robotic, not really engaged.

After church, I was left to deal with my thoughts. I could not muster up a prayer or read my Bible. Before this had happened to me, I had felt like I was finally starting to *flow* in the things of God. I was at church four times a week, attending church services and prayer meetings. I spent my daily time with God at home. Now to pray and read Scriptures reminded me of the abuse.

Instead of being spiritually empowered, I had seen the enemy steal my power. Like some victims of trauma, I found myself using the three-letter word *why*? You hear that word a lot in victim impact statements, when crime victims get an opportunity to speak at the sentencing of their attackers. Many times the offender doesn't offer an explanation. In wanting to know the reason for a person's actions, we must first be ready to handle the response. The explanation might re-victimize you emotionally.

As for me, I know that it is the Lord who searches the heart, and He knows the thoughts and the intentions of each person. I can speculate forever. I'm confident that I heard God say that a spirit of manipulation was present. I thank God that I am no longer trying to figure out why; it is more important for me to be free. If you're like I was, stop beating yourself up. Stop trying to analyze the situation. The Bible says that our trials work our patience. God can takes our hurt and pain, and use it to mold a ministry within us.

Co-founder Samantha Nelson of Hope for Survivors tells her account of spiritual abuse and how God brought healing to her and her husband:

> IS: What was going on in your life at the time of the abuse? Did you have an emotional need?

> SN: My husband and I had returned to church. We had our own business and were under a lot of stress. I had a lot of health problems at the time and was struggling to find a doctor who could properly diagnose and treat me. The pastor and his family became like family to us, which helped to meet our need for a spiritual father. The pastor

was 27 years older than me and, not having a close relationship with my biological father or my stepfather, having a spiritual father seemed to be a good thing.

IS: How did you feel each time you went to church and heard him preach, knowing what he was doing to you?

SN: That's a difficult question because he had created a set of hand signals for me to watch for as he preached. Each one meant something between us, like "I love you" or something like that. His sermons changed and he started directing them at me and my husband in the sense that we were manipulated into thinking God was telling us certain things which, of course, God wasn't saying at all. There were times I would listen to the pastor and think, what a hypocrite! Mostly, though, I was deeply ashamed of what was happening and wished that things could be *normal*—as in, he would be a good pastor and leave me alone (sexually).

IS: At what point did you decide to tell your husband?

SN: I wanted to tell my husband many times, but was afraid he might leave me. I felt I needed to keep this secret to myself—for everyone's sake—and I mistakenly thought I could handle it on my own, meaning end the relationship and make the pastor leave me alone.

My husband found out various things at different times during the abuse. He could sense something was wrong with me. I was acting unusual and talking about suicide, hurting myself again, etc. That wasn't who I was, so he knew something was wrong. He suspected the pastor was doing something to me and confronted me. I confessed, in part, to something the pastor had done, and Steve confronted the pastor who promised it would never happen again. Obviously, that was a lie. Steve found out the real truth when he discovered some information on my computer—information I had deleted at the pastor's instruction yet the Lord saw fit to make it accessible to Steve. At that time, Steve confronted me and the pastor again. Steve knew it was abuse from the beginning, which was a real blessing for me. He kept trying to help me see it as abuse.

IS: Had you realized that you didn't need the pastor, and what he was doing wrong?

SN: No, the pastor had me convinced that I would die without him. He had been counseling me (supposedly!) for some past abuse issues but, in reality, all he did was use that information to gain greater access to and control over me. I knew what he was doing was wrong—and pleaded with him not to pressure me, not to do what he wanted to do. I never wanted to have a sexual relationship with him at all, but he kept telling me God wanted us to be together; God would forgive; he needed me; I needed him; etc. Even after the sexual abuse ended, there was such spiritual and emotional damage, that part of me still felt I would die without the pastor in my life somehow. The truth is, the pastor had usurped the place of Jesus in my life and made me dependent upon him, not Jesus—something he never had a right to do.

IS: Do you think that you would have eventually turned him in had his wife not said anything?

SN: Given my emotional state at the time, that's difficult to say. I was trying to commit suicide every moment I was alone. I can't even count the number of times I tried and the Lord intervened through Steve. God was not going to allow me to die! I do believe that Steve would probably have turned him in at some point if the pastor's wife hadn't done so, and I think I would have come to that point in time too.

IS: You turned to your pastor seeking guidance and solace for the issues that you were dealing with, share with readers how you felt to be re-victimized.

SN: I said *no* many times, but it never seemed to mean anything to him. He knew, from our counseling sessions, that I had been gang-raped and was so terrified of being raped again that I felt I would just give in and go along with it if I was ever threatened. That way, I reasoned in my mind, I wouldn't have to face being forced. Knowing this information, the pastor kept pressuring me until I gave in, even though I was pleading with him to stop and saying *no* the whole time.

IS: Can you tell me how long did it take you to get over it, and what was your process. Did you go to counseling?

SN: It took several months to get over the emotional attachment. The pastor had been very good at manipulating and controlling my mind and actions. Steve and I had counseling, individually and as a couple, for a brief time, but didn't find it that helpful. In fact, one of my counselors asked me if I liked what was happening, which absolutely horrified and offended me, so I never went back to that one. Another didn't seem to recognize the professional exploitation and only became concerned when the pastor began stalking me. Truly, if Steve and I had listened to our counselors then, we would not be together today.

Only God deserves the credit and glory for the healing that took place in our lives, because He alone is the One who did it. After the sexual abuse ended, and after I had had surgery and was home recovering for several months, I began taking some Christian counseling classes (through correspondence school) so I could see for myself what the Bible said about abuse. Taking those courses got me back into my Bible, and being back in my Bible helped me get closer to Jesus. Being closer to Jesus is what enabled Him to heal me and my marriage. God did a wonderful work in our lives. The abuse ended in 2000, and we healed for the next couple of years. We never thought to start The Hope of Survivors. In fact, we had other thoughts and plans for different types of ministry. However, the Lord impressed

Steve that we needed to make truth available to others who were searching, as Steve had had difficulty finding truth to share with me. He told me what he was impressed to do, and we began writing and developing the website. We honestly never expected it to become a full-blown ministry with representatives and clients around the world, taking all my time and that of many other volunteers as well. We thought if we could help "just one," then our pain would have been worth going through, but God knew there were hundreds, indeed thousands, of just one's out there.

IS: How long was it for when you were finally able to feel like you could trust another pastor again?

SN: Steve and I learned a very valuable lesson through this. We learned that we should never give blanket (or automatic) trust to pastors just because of their profession. Trust, like respect, should be earned. A person—yes, even a pastor— must prove they are trustworthy before they should receive our trust. It took time to trust pastors and spiritual leadership again. We pray for spiritual discernment daily and believe God has given us that, which helps us to know who to trust and who not to trust.

IS: What do you say to people who aren't as close to God as others know the difference between a real man/woman of God and someone who is using manipulative means for selfish gain?

SN: The best advice I have is for people to read and know the Bible for themselves. That way, they will have the power and influence of the Holy Spirit in their lives and He will help them to discern between a true under-shepherd and a hireling or worse—a wolf in sheep's clothing. Only by knowing the Bible better, can anyone see when someone is acting out of harmony with the Word of God. If the pastor doesn't reveal Christ in his life, if he isn't patient, loving, tender, trustworthy, honest, meek, etc., then God is not with him. This becomes evident when you see self-glorification, selfishness, deceit, violation of God's commandments, control, irritability, anger, etc., in the pastor's life. Those things are not of God.

CHAPTER 5

My Journey

It is good to have an end to journey toward; but

it is the journey that matters, in the end.

—Ernest Hemingway

A journey is either the distance to be traveled or the time required for such a trip. Telling someone is the beginning of the journey to recovery. I confided in a friend and she pleaded with me to tell the senior pastors. I was reluctant, because I was not clear about what had happened and I didn't want any trouble. I was protecting Pastor Sale, but I ended up telling another associate pastor. Ultimately Pastor Sale was confronted and he confessed.

Despite claiming that he had only wanted to see me healed, he was removed from his position.

My road to healing led me down roads that I wanted to avoid, such as Anger Avenue, Trust Trail, Fear Inner Belt, and Forgiveness Highway. To move forward, I had to allow myself to recognize and acknowledge those feelings. There were no shortcuts.

Attempting to take control and liberate myself from my abuser, I began to self-destruct. Everything that he told me not to do, I did. I was feeding every part of my flesh, trying to fill the emptiness. The pastor told me to change my diet; I began to overeat. He said not to let anyone but him give me a massage; I went to the spa. I took things further. If I was going to have someone rub oil on me, I should get some gratification out of it. The enemy planted the seed, and I gave it a lot of thought. I met a man I liked, and although he and I did not have intercourse, I welcomed his embrace. For me he acted as an eraser, removing the pastor's fingerprints that had once tarnished my body. Psychologically I felt free because the pastor's hands weren't the last hands to touch my body.

According to RAINN, the chronic psychological consequences of rape or abuse include, but are not limited to, depression, attempted or completed suicide, cutting, alienation, unhealthy diet-related behaviors, high-risk sexual behavior, including unprotected sex, early sexual initiation, choosing unhealthy sexual partners, and having multiple sexual partners. An inability to maintain healthy relationships is also typical.

When the above behaviors get to the point where the person is experiencing feelings of hopelessness/helplessness, intrusive thoughts, detachment, hypervigilance, and/or exaggerated startle response, that person may have post-traumatic stress disorder.

Perhaps you are feeling some psychosomatic symptoms from the stress: headaches, stomachaches, or muscle tension. To help restore your nervous system to pre-trauma state, you can start by exercising. When the body is moving, it detoxes stress-produced chemicals such as cortisol. Surrounding yourself with a good support system increases your chances of recovery. Challenge feelings of helplessness by finding your voice. When you share your experience, you contribute to helping someone else, which helps you as well. If your symptoms continue, you may need to seek a professional therapist trained in evidence-based therapies such as Trauma-Focused Cognitive Behavior Therapy (TF-CBT) or Eye Movement Desensitization and Reprocessing (EMDR).

Anger Avenue

I remember the day that I told my support group I was angry. "Yes," I heard. "Thank goodness." It was okay for me to travel down this road, as long as I didn't live there. The Bible says that anger rests in the bosom of fools.

Victims of abuse need to work through the anger. Anger is only the tip of the iceberg. Underneath the anger are other feelings that need to be addressed: hurt, shame, humiliation, or rejection. My anger was displaced. Sure, I was angry with myself and people who made insensitive comments, but I was also angry with God. I was struggling with *God said*. The pastor had been confident that he knew the voice of the Lord—that he knew what *God said*.

My understanding of being a conduit for God didn't come until a year later. The Devil is the father of lies. Once we begin to operate in the flesh, we can confuse the voice of the Lord with our own selfish desires. Everything must line up with the Word of God. If something causes confusion, fear, or doubt, it is not of God.

First John 4:1 *(MSG)* says, "My dear friend, don't believe everything you hear. Carefully weigh or examine what people tell you. Not everyone who talks about God comes from God.

There are a lot of lying preachers loose in the world." I had to get to a place where I appropriately aimed my anger, and that meant aiming it toward the pastor. Notice that I previously mentioned being mad only at myself, insensitive people, and God. I still had to face the facts: this pastor had been in a position of power, and he had known the church rules.

Many people think that it is wrong to say you are mad at God, as if He doesn't already know your thoughts. The Bible says that He comprehends your ways. God's feelings aren't hurt when you express your feelings. It's egotistical of us to think that we have the ability to offend an omnipresent, omnificent God.

He wants you to confess your feelings so that you can be made whole. Sometimes we feel a righteous indignation, and that's okay. God understands and allows us to vent, cry, and fuss. When we are finished, His sweet Spirit comforts us. "Let us come boldly to the throne of grace that we may obtain mercy and find grace to help in time of need" (Hebrews 4:16 *NKJV*).

When channeled in a positive way, anger can bring about great results. Much legislation and many programs have been developed out of someone's anger toward the system. My anger toward God shut down my communion with Him. I didn't realize it at the time, but that was the enemy's intention. The enemy silenced the very thing that I would need to be victorious: my prayers. My spiritual pipes were clogged with anger, but worship is a very powerful tool. In time, I was able to sing about the characteristics of God, slowly flushing out the anger

Trust Trail

The calling of a teacher/preacher is not an easy job. The Bible says, James 3:1 "Not many of you should become teachers, my fellow believers, because you know that we who teach will be judged more strictly." God has set the standards higher for those in position. A leader's sentence will not be based on his achievements or how many members he obtained, or the programs implemented. God is going to hold teachers/pastors accountable as to how they use their influence.

Preachers often quote this passage: "Touch not my anointed and do my prophets no harm" (Psalm 105:15). In an abusive situation, this Scripture is usually a warning to the flock to keep them from talking against the pastor or others in leadership positions. We are to keep our lips from speaking evil about anyone and we are to respect leadership. Hebrews 13:17 says, "Obey your leaders and submit to their authority. They keep watch over you as men who must give an account. Obey them so that their work may be a joy and not a burden, for that would be of no advantage to you."

The Bible warns us about division and exclusion. Jesus said in Mark 9:42 that if anyone causes one of these little ones who believe in Him to stumble or to be offended, it would be better for him if a millstone were hung around his neck and thrown into the sea.

Our God is about order, and He has laid out in His Word how the church is to be structured. Both those in leadership and laymen are responsible for engaging in the kind of dialogue that builds trust. We are to lift pastors and other leaders up in prayer and submit to them. First Peter 5:2 says to serve as overseers not because you must, but because you are willing, as God wants you to be; not greedy for money, but eager to serve; not lording it over those entrusted to you, but by examples to the flock. First Timothy 5 1:1-2 gives us an outline of how church members should be treated: "do not rebuke an older man harshly, but exhort him as if he were your father. Treat younger men as brothers, older women as mothers, and younger women as sister, with absolute purity."

Spirituality is the most tender and easily wounded aspect of self. When trust is broken in clergy, the God image and a person's sacred interior is deeply wounded. Psychologist Stephen J. Rossetti believes that clergy are the image bearers for the Divine. They are seen as God's representatives and ambassadors. As Rossetti says, "When clergy abuse the power entrusted to them, that abuse is different from the abuse by any other professional. When clergy acts in abusive ways, the image of the Divine is shattered."

In a 2015 Gallup Poll, fewer than half of Americans said that they hold high regard for the church. Over the last decade our confidence in the church has declined. Misconduct in the church, as well as an increase in people identifying as nonreligious or non-Christian, may be contributing to that decline.

In trying to understand the disconnection between the church and the community, I surveyed one hundred people and asked these questions:

- With whom would you consult in a time of crisis?
- How well does your spiritual leader know you?
- How often do you attend religious services?

Did attending a religious service weekly correlate to how well the spiritual leader knew the member? Eighty people out of a hundred reported that they would consult with family or friends in a time of crisis. Thirty out of a hundred people said they attended organized religious services weekly, and the majority of those surveyed reported their spiritual leader knowing them somewhat or not at all.

When we speak of our spirit, we are then God conscious. When abuse happens, or we develop mistrust in leadership, it can cause us to question our beliefs and values. Patricia L. Liberty, a contributing writer to *When a Congregation Is Betrayed*, says that authentic spiritual healing grows out of pain, sadness, confusion, anger, rage, and feelings of hopelessness. Liberty writes that grief makes up a large part of the work that a victim must do. As explained in a previous chapter, the stages of grief are denial, anger, bargaining, depression, and acceptance.

The image of God needs to be reshaped. Many times the abuser uses God language to justify his actions, making it confusing to the victim. In my case, I was told, "God can trust you" or "God wants you to be my armor bearer." Questions arise such as "How can a loving God give so much power and influence to a man whom He knew would be abusive?"

Jeremiah 6:14 says, "They dress the wound of my people as though it were not serious. 'Peace, Peace' they say, when there is no peace." The work of the church in helping those who have been hurt is acknowledgment. The church has to be sensitive to that person's journey. Laypeople who have been abused by leadership may not want to return to an institution where they don't feel supported. During this time of recovery, the victim needs that connection to

God and also to people of like faith. So how do we bridge the two? Provide active listening, be empathetic, and exercise the ministry of presence. You can do this by making a phone call, inviting the person out to lunch, or asking the person if he or she would like company. You can offer to pray with the person, or to take Communion with you. Taking Communion will help bring the person back to the cross, the message of God's grace for each person. Remember to meet people where they are in their journey.

A congregation, as a system, is a community of people who hold something in common. In many cultures, church is seen as an extension of our nuclear family. The Latin word for family is *familia*, which means "household." In the book of Acts, we read that when the church began, people gathered, shared their goods, and served one another.

Just as you have rules in your household, the church has rules. In her book *Understanding Clergy Misconduct in Religious Systems*, Candace Benyei writes about four types of rules:

- Formal rules: These are guidelines or published bylaws.
- Informal rules: These rules tell us, for example, to stand up during altar call, not to walk around while someone is

praying or reading a Scripture, or to raise your forefinger to excuse yourself during a service.

- Implicit rules: These are unwritten rules that the congregation unconsciously follows. These rules have been modeled and repeated, passed down through the generations, perhaps from the leadership's family of origin. "Do as I say," and "Get behind your leaders." It's easy for a congregation to adapt to these principles without even being aware of it. Benyei says, "It's like wallpaper, members are careful not to deface it for fear of rejection or disapproval."

- The rule of secrecy: Sometimes leaders or members of the church have experienced events in their lives that they perceive as shameful. When something bad happens— something that is a disadvantage to the church—those people will want to suppress the knowledge of that event or refrain from talking about it. The church members may have been given a gag order by the church leaders. Keeping secrets is also a means of maintaining a position of power.

Many families have a sense of loyalty. Loyalty is defined by Merriam-Webster Dictionary as "the state or quality or an instance of being loyal. It is a strong feeling of support for someone or something." The downside to being loyal in a family or church is that sometimes it leads to condoning wrongful behavior. The church will tolerate abuse for the greater good of the church, such as keeping a pastor who has engaged in wrongful behavior but is considered charismatic. Churches sometimes have a strong desire to abide by the anti-conflict rule of "Don't rock the boat."

Allegiance to a church is a choice, just as it is in families. However, some families have ways to coerce members into being supportive, perhaps by means of a threat. For example, "If you let your sister get beat up, you will get in trouble when you get home." The message is that as a family, we either stick together or we get reprimanded. In church, people are punished by being shunned. Church members can be ostracized for anything from wearing pants to church to questioning the funding of the church to revealing that a church leader has abused his power. The resultant shunning can cause inner turmoil, therefore leading to a person's spiritual death.

Trusting people in positions of power will take time. Develop trust slowly, being fully aware of your emotional and spiritual needs. Watch and pray. Ask God to give you the wisdom to know when to open the door and allow the right people into your life, and when to disclose personal information about yourself. Keep in mind that not all pastors and leaders are bad, and that some men and women of God are trustworthy.

Fear Inner Belt

Fear, like shame, can serve as an inner alarm to protect us. Many times victims experience fear of the perpetrator, fear of abandonment, or fear of harm from other people. Victims sometimes fear the unknown, and wonder how they can exist after the abuse.

Fear keeps you in bondage. Instead of dealing with the abuse, many people compensate by overeating; isolating themselves; staying busy; abusing drugs, sex, and/or alcohol; minimizing the problem; or becoming perfectionists.

When my church fired the pastor who had abused me, I wasn't afraid that he would physically harm me. It wasn't until I started to experience pain in my body that fear gripped me. What if God had told him to anoint me with oil?

The enemy was telling me that the pastor had put a spell on me. What I didn't understand was that a spirit had been sent to torment my mind. The enemy wanted me to focus on my physical symptoms, rather than on the fact that Jesus had already healed me. The Devil had a strong hold on me. In Greek, *stronghold* is defined as a demonically induced thought. The only way to destroy it is with the spoken Word of God. The Bible tells us to do away with every thought that puts itself above what we know about Jesus Christ. We have to gather up the thought and restrain it, replacing every negative thought with the promises of God.

Shortly after the dismissal of the pastor, I began to feel restless in my home. I felt like a stranger had invaded my house, and the stench of the intruder was still lingering. I knew that in the spiritual realm, something had transpired. My fear was that my purpose had been aborted. I feared not being able to emerge with my sanity and salvation.

I was constantly looking over my shoulder. A few times while sitting in church, I thought I saw him. Fear was taking hold of my mind, and I became hypervigilant. I had recurring nightmares of being in a closed space, unable to escape the pastor coming toward me. The chill from my sweat-soaked nightgown would awaken me. It took time and the prayers of people I knew—and some I did not know—for those dreams to cease.

It is human nature to experience the emotion of fear. However, you cannot allow fear to keep you from living your life. Satan's plan is to kill, steal, and destroy. If you're reading this, then the enemy has not accomplished what he set out to do to you. It was on my heart that if I knew what the Devil wanted to do to me, I would give God the praise. Whatever intentions the enemy had for you, to be achieved through the abuse, they will not prosper.

Now I realize that I had put my trust in man, when I actually needed to look to the Lord for my help. I needed to get the Word deep down inside me, so that when the enemy caused me to experience physical pain, I would have the shield of faith and the sword—the Word of God—to protect me. If things had continued the way they were going, every time I had a pain or wanted direction from God, I would have gone to the pastor. The pastor had taken over God's place, but we are never supposed to esteem man higher than God. It is God who works through man.

As I mentioned before, there are times when the emotion of fear serves to warn us of impending danger. If you fear for your life, I encourage you to seek out professional help. Don't announce to your abuser what you are planning to do—just do it. Many times the abuser will use fear to keep you silent with threats, such as "I will hurt you and your family" or "No one will believe you."

Psalm 27:1–3 *(NKJV)* says, "The Lord is my light and my salvation; whom shall I fear? The Lord is the strength of my life, whom shall I be afraid? When the wicked came against me to eat up my flesh, my enemies and foes, they stumbled and fell. Though an army may encamp against me, my heart shall not fear; though war may rise against me, in this I will be confident."

Forgiveness Highway

Forgiving someone is a very powerful gesture. Holding back forgiveness for other people hinders us from receiving forgiveness from God when we sin. I marvel at how families of crime victims can stand in court and say to the suspect that they forgive him or her. I know that there are stages of grief, so when those family members feel angry, who is that anger directed toward: the suspect, themselves, or God? When they feel anger, does that mean they haven't really forgiven the person? Although I don't profess to be an expert in forgiveness, as a Christian I can only go by what the Word of God says about forgiveness. In my humanness, I ask God for His grace to do what His Word instructs me to do.

Not forgiving hinders our prayers. Mark 11:24 encourages us to believe that we already have that for which we are petitioning God in prayer. Then verse 25 says, "Whenever you stand praying, if you have anything against anyone, forgive him." These verses imply that answered prayers are contingent upon us having faith and forgiveness.

Forgiving is the last thing a person who has been raped, molested, or harassed wants to hear about. However, forgiveness isn't about your abuser—it's about you. To forgive your abuser doesn't mean that what you feel is any less painful, or that you are denying the reality of what happened. On the contrary, by forgiving your abuser, you take the power back into your own hands.

The Greek meaning for forgiveness is "to send away." When you forgive, you send that person away from your mind and emotions. By forgiving, you release the power that your abuser once had over you. When you forgive, you don't waste time wishing ill toward your abuser, and he no longer consumes your thoughts. You do, however, continue to seek justice.

Several months after my abuse, I went to a church service. The speaker called me out of the audience, so I reluctantly went up to the stage. He told me to say aloud that I forgave the person who had hurt me. My first thought was, *I do not trust this speaker. Why would I say that I forgive my abuser, when I am still feeling so empty inside?* I complied, perhaps only because of the implicit rule to respond when asked to do so by the speaker. But for whatever reason, I heard myself say that I forgave my abuser. And when I spoke those words that prepared the atmosphere in the spiritual realm for positive change to take place in my life.

Forgiving someone who has abused you takes time. But if you step out on faith and give it to Jesus, He will begin to peel back the layers of hurt and anger. God designed this body to heal itself. When you cut yourself, you bleed and feel pain. Usually you wash the cut and put ointment on it. In a few days, the cut begins to heal.

Depending on how deep the cut was, there might be a scar, but the pain is gone. Looking at the scar may remind you of the accident, but the pain that you experienced at that time is no longer there.

So it is in the Spirit. When we get hurt, we go to God with our pain. He washes it with the shed blood of Jesus Christ. He applies His healing balm, the Holy Ghost, to your wound. And in time, your scar will become your witness that you are more than a conqueror in Christ Jesus.

I knew that God had begun a healing process in me when I could openly talk about what happened and not feel distressed. I no longer got upset when I saw his family. In time, I began to pray blessings over his life and the lives of people connected to him.

Forgiving a person does not mean that you will forget. Sometimes when you hear a song, see a movie, or hear about abuse, your mind will return to the event and you'll experience some of those old feelings. This is called *object relation*. Early in my journey, when I saw any kind of oil, my stomach would tighten, because the oil reminded me of what happened with the pastor. It didn't matter if it was cooking oil, massage oil, or motor oil. I just did not want it near me.

Remember, this journey takes time. Don't try to rush the process. You don't want pseudo-feelings, for the sake of being a good Christian. In her book *How Can I Forgive You?* Janis Abrahms Spring writes about the courage to forgive in your relationships and the freedom not to. In her book, she explains cheap forgiveness. You may be thinking, *What is cheap forgiveness?* Cheap forgiveness is an easy way of dealing with a violation without processing any emotions. As Spring explains, "It's a compulsive, unconditional, unilateral attempt at peacemaking for which you ask nothing in return."

Spring suggests that by forgiving cheaply, you rob yourself of the possibility of developing a more intimate bond with the offender. When an offense has occurred and it is not talked about, nothing is resolved. The offender is not held accountable for his actions, and healing does not take place within the relationship.

Cheap forgiveness blocks personal growth. When you forgive too quickly, you don't allow yourself to learn from your own complexities. Cheap forgiveness gives the impression to the offender that his actions were okay. Cheap forgiveness can make you physically and emotionally sick. By not allowing yourself to be upset, you deny yourself the opportunity to feel hostility and anger.

Rely on God to help you to forgive. Authentic forgiveness has to be done by the Spirit of God. The Bible says that in the flesh dwells no good thing. Outside of ourselves, we cannot forgive those who have hurt us. This is why we must ask for God's help.

CHAPTER 6

Pressing Forward

Am I in the Place of God? You intended to harm me
but God intended it for good to accomplish what
is now being done, the saving of many lives.

—Genesis 50:19–20

My healing is a continuum. I feel a pressing, which implies there is a force, an object in front of me. I would like to say that I now fully trust pastors and that I know why my abuse took place, but I don't. As one of my college professors so wisely told me, I have to learn to be comfortable with the incomplete. There will be situations in which we will never see the result—people whom we have counseled, a relationship, or a project. The good thing about something being incomplete is that it leaves room for growth. As I push past fear, shame, and anger in various areas of my life, I am growing.

Another chapter of my life has yet to be revealed to me. God, the author, has already written my life script. He knows all the people I will encounter in my life, and when that will happen. God knows the antagonistic who represents the obstacles in my life, and the minor characters who will come on the scene to help develop my story. God has already positioned me for the second half of my life.

Several years after my experience with the pastor, I returned to the church where I was born and raised. They were in transition, looking for a new pastor. I settled back into my old routine of sitting in the back of the church, arriving late and leaving early. I watched and wondered, where was I to serve? Was praying, teaching, and counseling only for a season?

My current pastor and his wife have a love for souls. I appreciate the fact that they understand that trust is not automatic. With the help of the Lord, it is possible to trust again. Remember, a journey is the time it takes to get to a particular place. Each one of us has an established, divine time for our journeys through life.

Deliverance

To be delivered means "to give over to." When I acknowledged what had happened to me, I knew that I needed prayer. The Bible teaches us, through examples, that there are times to pray for deliverance and to renounce the spirit that once bound you.

Although I went to counseling, I wanted to be totally free from this pastor and other men who had been abusive in my life. An associate female pastor and my mentor came to my house and prayed for me and my home, which still felt as though it had been invaded.

I asked God to help me forgive myself and see myself as He sees me. I realize that during that season in my life, I had many regrets. I'd been very critical of myself. In learning more about spirits and demonic activity, I realized that my body was turning on me the same way I had turned on myself. What was going on in my soul had a great effect on my physical body. The stress of everything caused my immune system to begin to attack healthy cells.

Instead of enjoying where I was in Christ, and trusting that God was ordering my steps, I abused myself with negative thoughts: *You don't have any gifts. You aren't anointed. God won't talk to you.* Amos 3:3 says, "How can two walk together unless they agree?" I had to learn what the Bible said about me. I had to uproot that which had been planted in me as a child.

In any kind of deliverance, we must do certain things to remain delivered. I'm reminded of the story in Matthew 12:43–45. "When an evil spirit comes out of a man, it goes through arid places seeking rest and does not find it. Then it will say, 'I will return to the house I left.' When it returns, it finds the house unoccupied, swept clean and put in order. Then it goes and takes with it seven other spirits more wicked than itself and they go in and live there. And the final condition of that man is worse than the first. That is how is will be with this wicked generation."

So many of us get prayed over, and afterward feel empowered and invigorated. But what happens when we go back home? We know that God has touched our lives. Like the man in this passage from Matthew, our souls were emptied and cleaned, but we haven't filled them with anything positive. Our victory is short-lived.

Once we have been delivered, we have a responsibility to stay delivered. We do this by renewing our minds daily with the Word of God. For some of us, it may mean letting go of old friends or no longer going to the same places where we used to go. Two opposing forces cannot coexist in the same place.

Carolo DiClemente and James O. Prochaska developed a psychological model called the Stages of Change, which includes pre-contemplation, contemplation, determination, action, and maintenance. Let's say you are in a destructive relationship. Most of the time, your significant other is nice and showers you with gifts. At other times, however, he isolates you from your family. Well-meaning friends have told you that you deserve better. At first, you believe they are overreacting and perhaps are even jealous because you are in a relationship.

Time passes, and you start to think about how he pushes you and berates you. You begin to consider leaving the destructive relationship, but you hesitate because of all the time you have invested in it.

One day, the two of you go out to dinner together, and he spends the entire time criticizing your dress, talking about how much food you are eating, and overtly flirting with the waitress right in front of you. When you get home, he demands that you do sexual favors for him, reminding you that many women would love to be his lady.

Now in the determination phase of change, you have an epiphany. You begin to realize your self-worth. You are ready to make the necessary changes in your life. You break off the relationship and get a new phone number. You stop going to places that he frequented. You realize that you are better off without him. As you do some introspection, you see more clearly your pattern of behavior when it comes to relationships and the type of men you attract. You solicit the help of family and friends to help you be accountable in staying out of that relationship. Sometimes when you are alone, your mind goes back to moments you shared with him. This is the time to reach out to friends and acknowledge how you are feeling.

He catches you at a vulnerable time and you temporarily relapse right back into his arms, but that's okay. According to the stages, you may want to revisit contemplation or determination. Now you have reached the termination stage, where you do less relapsing and ruminating over the relationship. You have identified your triggers, and you are using your accountability partners. You have found your self-worth. You are enjoying your newfound freedom.

We experience dissonance when we are not being the person we want to be. Part of changing has something to do with chemicals in our brain. Cells in our brain release and request information. If we continue to experience dissonance, our brain will release the chemical cortisol and those cells will multiply, asking for more cells to seek out the behavior and feeling that cortisol provides.

Apostle Paul knew what it meant to experience two opposing feelings at the same time:

> For what I am doing, I do not understand. For what I will to do, that I do not practice; but what I hate, that I do. If, then I do what I will not to do, I agree with the law, that it is good. But now, it is no longer I who do it, but sin that dwells in me. For I know that in me (that is my flesh) nothing good dwells; for to will is present with me, but how to perform what is good I do not find. For the good that I will to do, I do not do, but the evil I will not to do, that I practice. (Romans 7:15–19 *[NKJV]*).

Paul understood that he could not be bound to the law, and that it was only by the grace of God that he was able to do what was required of him.

Confrontation

I'd like to briefly discuss the importance of confrontation. Some people have the misconception that confrontation means "to have a disagreement or an argument." However, confronting a friend, parent, spouse, or coworker can be very beneficial for both parties.

In the case of abuse, sometimes the victim can address the abuser through a process called *actual confrontation.* The victim is generally advised not to expect contrition on the part of the abuser. Many times the abuser denies the whole thing, leaving the victim feeling frustrated, hurt, and confused. At other times, it is not safe or practical to confront the abuser because of danger or the person being deceased. The empty chair approach is a Gestalt technique that can be used to process unfinished business. The victim can visualize the abuser sitting in the chair and express her feelings in a safe environment. Some victims may choose to do storytelling and narrative therapy, which is a component in Trauma-Focused Cognitive Behavior Therapy.

If you prefer to actually confront your abuser, you need to first pray. I also advise you to take someone with you, rather than going alone. Go into it with the idea that the confrontation is for you—not for him. And again, don't expect the perpetrator to be remorseful.

I wanted to confront Pastor Sale. I wanted to see him for myself, so that I would know that my fear was gone. Once when I thought that I saw his parked car, I drove close to it and felt my heart beat rapidly. Would I stop and say something? Would I be able to control my foot on the accelerator? I drove by slowly and just looked at him from a distance. After that, I dreamed several times that I saw him in public places. In one of my dreams, I did get a chance to express how his actions affected my life. It was so surreal that I woke up with tears in my eyes.

As of today, I have not gotten a chance to actually talk to him about what took place. But what do you say to someone who admits his actions and yet feels strongly that he was being obedient to God? Forgiveness is an act of faith. I reflected on how fear had gripped me, especially at night. As I began to pray for his family, I had more dreams. In one dream, I saw him with his wife, and the next morning, I woke up rejoicing because I knew that I had forgiven him. In that particular dream, I was walking toward him and saying hello.

That dream became reality a year later. My day started with no particular agenda, but then I decided that I needed to go to the store. My car seemed to be on autopilot, because I ended up at the store closest to my house—a location that I don't usually patronize. I entered the store and walked over to the aisle where the items for which I was looking were located. As I turned to go down the aisle, standing six feet in front of me was Pastor Sale and his wife. My dream was being played out. I walked in his direction and said hello, and he looked at me, nodded, and walked past me. I was so overcome with joy that I left the cart, still containing my shopping items, and walked out of the store. I could feel God's presence surrounding me, and I began to cry, raising my hands as a sign of victory.

I immediately called my mentor to tell her that I had seen him. I'm sure she couldn't understand me, because audibly I didn't make sense. In the middle of my explanation, I would twirl around and cry. I was not aware of the fact that I was on the sidewalk of a crowded parking lot. After years of torment and nightmares, I was free, praise God! There was no need to make any conversation. My confrontation with him was having the courage to face him. I just put one foot in front of the other and moved forward, beginning a new chapter in my life.

Like Joseph in the Bible, I have to say that, yes, I am in the place of God. He has done so much for me, and as a result of what I went through, I am a stronger person in Him. I will no longer look to people to be what only God can be to me. It is God who has called me, who has gifted me, and who validates who I am in the kingdom of God.

CONCLUSION

God has given each of us things for which to be responsible. If we don't understand or treasure the purpose of those things, then we can abuse them. Abuse—whether sexual, verbal, physical, or spiritual—can have long-lasting effects on a person's perception of herself and her life. Only through Jesus Christ can a person truly be restored.

The first step is accepting what happened and breaking the silence by sharing your feelings with someone. Remember that people may get impatient and give you a schedule for getting over a situation, but you should never feel that you can't go to God as many times as you need.

Restoring trust in the institution that represents your abuse will mean challenging some distorted thoughts, appropriately placing responsibility, allowing yourself to feel emotions, and having some form of confrontation. Ask God for discernment to recognize the true intentions of a person's actions. Trust the God in you. God is constantly speaking to us; we just need to be still in the center of our core and acknowledge Him.

Understand the origin of your shame and begin to discuss it with your social supports. Allow yourself time to work through the shame, guilt, fear, and anger. Don't feel pressured by other people's expectations that you should stay strong. Listening to these messages may hinder you from giving yourself permission to feel whatever emotions you are experiencing.

Stay connected. Don't isolate yourself. Surround yourself with people who can uphold you during your time of healing. No situation is insignificant to God. Perhaps the abuse you experienced was not as overt as sexual abuse, but you know that something happened that left you feeling discombobulated. I advise you to pray and ask for wisdom about how to get your concerns addressed.

I pray that this book has been a blessing to you. I would be remiss if I did not end with prayer, for it is through prayer that the gifts that God has placed inside of me come forth. I ask that God would help those who have been abused, whether emotionally, physically, sexually, or spiritually. I pray that God restores the seconds, minutes, and years that the enemy has stolen from you. I pray that God gives you a renewed sense of hope for life. I pray that He would bind up your wounds and heal your broken heart. I pray that your feelings of shame and guilt will be released, and that you receive blessings for the burdens you have carried and a song for your sorrow. I petition God on your behalf that He will rise up and that everything that tries to hinder you will be scattered as you begin your journey toward breaking your silence.

I pray for the families of victims of abuse. I ask the Lord to give them the wisdom and knowledge to handle the situation. I speak against fault finding, blame, denial, and regret, in the name of Jesus. I ask that what has happened in the dark be brought to light, and that family secrets be exposed. I ask, in Jesus's name, that each family member and friend will be supportive.

I pray for the abusers, whether they're parents, pastors, teachers, or friends. Many times abusers have been abused themselves. I pray that healing takes place in their lives. I pray that they will have humble and contrite spirits. I plead the blood of Jesus over their minds. I speak against their feelings of grandeur and their prideful spirits. I ask God to show them the error of their ways. I pray that they have clean hearts, standing on God's word that He is faithful and just to forgive and to cleanse all sin. I ask that God help their families, not to support them in wrongdoing, but to love them by holding them accountable for their actions. I ask that the scales from their eyes be removed and that they no longer walk in darkness, but into the light of God.

Lastly, I intercede on behalf of the church. I pray that we no longer operate as usual, as though spiritual abuse does not occur in our churches. I ask that pastors and leaders take a stance so that abuse in any form will no longer be tolerated. I pray that God grants wisdom to the church, to be able to lovingly minister to people who have been abused. And I pray for reconciliation between spiritual leaders and laymen.

May God bless every person whose hands hold this book, whether by way of purchase, gift, or happenstance. I ask that the anointing of the Holy Spirit permeate through the pages of this book and provoke change. I claim this and believe by faith in Jesus's name. Amen.

TRUST AGAIN

It took so much strength

Within

For me to trust again

I've been misused, abused

But somehow I will trust again

Because trust is time

Something so treasured and precious

With God's protection

I can gain it in seconds

It took time to trust you

So trust me

Trusting is easier said than done

And it takes time to build trust

His time isn't our time

So when the time comes

Your pain will be healed

And you will trust again

N.M. (age fifteen)

SOURCES

Benyei, Candace R. *Understanding Clergy Misconduct in Religious Systems: Scapegoating, Family Secrets, and the Abuse of Power.* Birmingham, AL: Haworth Pastoral Press, 1998.

Godwin, Alan. "Inside The Manipulator's Mind: The Insider's Guide to Ending Emotional Exploitation." Video series, 2015. Cross Country Education. www.crosscountryeducation.com.

Johnson, David, and Jeff VanVonderen. *The Subtle Power of Spiritual Abuse: Recognizing and Escaping Spiritual Manipulation and False Spiritual Authority Within the Church.* Minneapolis: Bethany House, 2005.

Kubetin, Cynthia, and James Mallory. *Shelter from the Storm: Hope for Survivors of Sexual Abuse.* Search Resources, 1995.

Potter-Efron, Ronald, and Patricia Potter-Efron. *Letting Go of Shame: Understanding How Shame Affects Your Life.* Hazelden, 1989.

Spring, Janis Abrahms. *How Can I Forgive You? The Courage to Forgive, the Freedom Not To.* New York: Harper Collins, 2004.

DISCUSSION QUESTIONS

- Has a situation in your church or community caused you to lose confidence in your religious organization?

- Do you feel comfortable talking to your pastor or spiritual leader about your concerns? Are there any areas that you do not feel comfortable discussing with your pastor or spiritual leader?

- The author gives examples of manipulative behavior. Discuss a time when you used manipulation. Discuss a time when you were manipulated.

- Discuss a time when you felt shame. What was the origin of the shame?

- The Bible instructs Christians to forgive. Think of a scenario in which it may be difficult for you to forgive someone.

ADDITIONAL RESOURCES

Hope for Survivors. www.hope4survivors.com.

National Suicide Prevention Lifeline. 1-800-273-TALK, ext. 8255.

Spiritual Abuse Recovery Resources. www.spiritualabuse.com.

Survivor Network of those Abused by Priests. www.snapnetwork.org.

This Journey. www.thisjourney.org

Young Women's Christian Association. www.ywca.com.

Printed in the United States
By Bookmasters